How
Tumors for a
Successful Pregnancy
Over 40

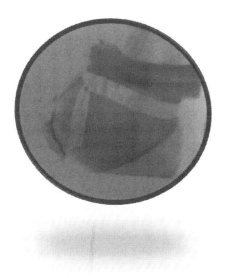

By Sandra K.
Jones-Keller

Also by Sandra Jones-Keller

Intuitive Communication With Your Baby's Soul

21 Lessons To Empower The New Age Kid

PREFACE

According to the Illinois Department of Public Health, as many as 77% of child-bearing women could have fibroid tumors and not even know it. I was one of those women.

I'm sharing my story to encourage and empower you! Having fibroid tumors does not automatically mean you can't get pregnant and/or have a healthy and successful pregnancy. My journey is proof of this. I dug into my spiritual toolbox to guide me through this miraculous process.

CONTENTS

IN THE BEGINNING

When I've told this story in the past it was all neat and packaged like store bought chicken that's already been plucked and pre-packed in clear wrap and Styrofoam. But my journey was more like visiting a slaughterhouse, messy, bloody and stressful and definitely not something I would ever want to encounter again.

I was 41 years old when I became pregnant and had only been with Thomas (my then boyfriend, now husband) for three months in the same city. We'd had a long distance relationship for 6 months prior to him moving in, but talking to someone on the phone was hella different than living with them. Our relationship was new, the pregnancy was unplanned, and my body was out of sorts.

Before I even went to the doctor, I knew something was awry. I was only a few days late with my cycle, but I looked like I was 3-4 months pregnant. Turns out I had a couple of large fibroid tumors, one of which was at the base of my uterus, completely obstructing my birth canal. My heart sank while dreams of a natural water birth shattered as quickly as a mirror dropping. The doctor's prognosis for me was pretty dire: I'd be bedridden for most of my pregnancy, Mecca would be born 3 months premature, and I would have a C-section. I didn't know any of this when we booked a two week vacation for the following month to the ancient Mayan ruins of Palenque, Mexico, immediately after my home pregnancy test came back positive.

I felt fantastic for most of our trip—better than I had in weeks. Being out of the country definitely agreed with me, I grew stronger and more balanced. I laughed and played and soaked in the healing energy of the sacred site. However, I over extended myself on a 2 day excursion to the beach and by the time we arrived back to our jungle cabin I was spotting blood.

Since there was no pain, I wasn't too concerned at first. I rested frequently while Thomas explored the ruins. But my anxiety increased as the spotting continued and I was trepidatious about our long bus ride into the city to catch our 6½ hour flight back to Los Angeles.

Given that we were in a quaint village in the Yucatan Peninsula, there weren't any walk-in clinics available to get a checkup. We were finally referred to a local mid-wife. I use the term mid-wife loosely—she had birthed 5 or 6 kids of her own and was considered knowledgeable in this area.

We tracked the mid-wife down at her job in a local cantina. Using lots of hand gestures and butchered Spanish, I explained my problem as we stood outside the back of the restaurant. She pointed to Thomas to grab a lone mattress that happened to be nearby (her mobile office perhaps?) then motioned for me to lie down on it. We were so desperate for help that we complied with no hesitation. She dug into my stomach for several minutes, feeling and sensing my womb. She concluded my baby was fine and I was okay to travel, although she insisted I was at least 4-5 months pregnant instead of just the 2 months that I was. Our language barrier prevented her from understanding my fibroids explanation. The next day, we had a safe and uneventful trip back to the states where I began regular checkups.

***

It was unsettling for me to have recurrent doctor's appointments; I preferred acupuncture and homeopathy to Western medicine. Now I was thrust into stirrups and ultrasounds, routine poking and prodding of my most intimate parts, long delays in beige colored waiting rooms, and well-meaning health care professionals predicting a disastrous future for my long-awaited pregnancy. I wanted to scream and often times did as soon as I left the sterile offices filled with glowing pregnant woman. Why wasn't I glowing and happy, I often wondered.

I was jealous and envious of the women who seemed to be 'doing' pregnancy a lot easier than me, and tired of crying after most of my appointments. I felt helpless and at the mercy of mainstream medicine which I had spent so many years avoiding.

Ultimately, I went back to basics and began treating my pregnancy like I would any other challenge or fear in my life: I got busier and deeper into my spiritual practices. I began meditating more. I spent time in quiet contemplation and reflection. I did spiritual mind treatments (affirmative prayer) with a practitioner and had energy healing sessions. I connected with nature, read my spiritual books, wrote out positive affirmations, and most of all, I listened deeply and intently to my intuition.

What ensued over the next 8 ½ months was a partnership between me and my unborn daughter to have a healthy and successful pregnancy. I did have a C-section, but I carried her full term. I was never bedridden. As a matter of fact, I worked part-time up until the weekend before she was born. And Mecca came home at the end of my hospital stay. How did I beat my prognosis? I developed intuitive two-way communication with my baby. I talked to my unborn daughter and she answered back! Yes, answered back!

THE FIRST TIME MECCA TALKED BACK TO ME

I was about three months pregnant the first time Mecca talked back to me. Thomas and I were at a spiritual conference in Las Vegas. We were scheduled to return to Los Angeles on Monday. What Thomas hadn't told me was that he had checked us out of our hotel room on Sunday and we were going to spend the last night with his friend (to save some money.) Well I was pregnant and uncomfortable and very annoyed. I didn't want to share a room with someone else, so I told him I would catch a ride back to Los Angeles. He totally surprised me by asking, "Did you ask Mecca what she wants to do?"

My first thought was, "Why do I need to ask her? It's my body, I get to decide." But I thought I would humor him. I went into meditation, quieted my mind and asked Mecca, "Do you want to go home with me or stay in Vegas with Daddy?" Before I barely finished the question, I heard a voice in my mind say, "I want to stay here with my daddy." Now this was not the answer I wanted! I had my own agenda, I wanted to go home and thought for sure that she would want to go with me. Not to be deterred, I asked her again—the same answer. I knew this was her voice because the answer wasn't what I intended and she said 'my daddy.' I went back to Thomas and begrudgingly said, "We're staying."

HOW I CREATED A PARTNERSHIP WITH MECCA AND MY BODY

After my first two-way telepathic (an internal voice I heard in my head) conversation with Mecca in Las Vegas, she and I had access to a deeper level of communication. Before this, I had been simply talking to her, rubbing my belly and loving her silently. Now I knew she could and would answer back!

I began to rely on her feedback and wisdom to support me during my pregnancy. Even though I was still apprehensive and often panicky after several of my doctor's appointments, I didn't feel helpless anymore.

When my doctor would say with complete confidence things like: "Mecca will be born early because your uterus can only stretch so far and you are pretty close to that maximum," or "There's a chance your fibroids might interfere with the growth of your baby,"

13

or "We can't find your baby's heartbeat," or "We have to run more tests, we think your kidney may be enlarged due to the extra stress on your body," I would cry and bemoan my difficult pregnancy, then ground myself and communicate with my daughter.

Almost daily I would ask Mecca how she was doing. Her answer was always the same, "I'm fine mom, take care of yourself." She had carved a space for herself in between my fibroids and was hanging out there contentedly. I could feel her strong, loving, confident energy ushering me along the way. Because I knew she was fine, I had the strength and willpower to focus on myself, doing what I needed to do to carry her safely to full-term.

In addition to creating a partnership with Mecca, I created a partnership with my body. I would tune into my body and ask if it needed more rest, or exercise or what type of foods would best support it. I was even guided to sit in the sauna for 10 minutes after my light swims. Everyone is different which is why it's critical to tap into your higher self and follow your own intuitive guidance. Some women may need exercise some may not, or you may actually need to be bedridden. But I knew I didn't need to be bedridden because I asked my daughter and I asked my body.

***

The most frightening part of the 38 weeks was the day of my delivery. I had a scheduled C-section first thing in the morning. The staff tested and retested my blood. They delayed taking me into the operating room. I could feel the fear and apprehension all around me. I realized the doctors were afraid of excessive bleeding during my procedure and were preparing for all possibilities.

I was terrified by the time Thomas entered the brightly lit room to join me for the birth of our baby girl. I grabbed his hand and requested he sing to me in my ear. We sang mindless Christmas carols throughout my delivery, trying to stay calm in the midst of the frightful energy engulfing the room like fog on a cool winter's morning. After what seemed like a lifetime of doctors yanking on my tummy, a nurse finally held my beautiful girl above the dividing curtain for me to see before whisking her away to be cleaned up and assessed. As we had previously agreed, Thomas went with Mecca while I remained on the table.

At some point, I consciously decided I was not going to bleed to death. I accessed a deep, trance-like meditation, unlike anything I had ever experienced before or since that moment—I literally left my body and focused on the vibration of life, wellness and motherhood. It wasn't until I heard the doctors say, "She's all clear," that I took a deep breath and reentered my physical being. My terror and will to live sparked my absolute determination. I concentrated only on surviving and being with my precious newborn! I was totally connected to her and could feel her strength even through this distress.

A HIGHER POWER

What the doctors didn't know that I knew was that there was a higher power than the medical profession that I was calling on throughout my high-risk pregnancy and delivery. I call it God, some may call it Spirit, Holy Spirit, Allah, Christ, angels; you may call it whatever is comfortable for you. This Universal Power completely supported and guided me on this journey.

I had tremendous medical care, nevertheless my doctors and nurses had based their conjectures on what they had seen in the past. Had I bought into the medical professional's experiences, then my original prognosis probably would have occurred. Fortunately, I had my spiritual toolbox to pull from which assisted me in creating a different reality than the predictions I had received.

A HYSTERECTOMY?

Another occurrence my doctor forecasted was that I would have to have a hysterectomy at some point since my grapefruit sized fibroid would likely cause pain and other complications. He didn't attempt to remove my female organs during my C-section for fear of severe bleeding, and because he wanted to focus solely on delivering Mecca safely, but suggested that I prepare for it in the near future. Even though I was done having children after my tumultuous pregnancy, I was still devastated. I didn't want any part of my body cut out for any reason.

Through muddled tears, I meditated and communicated with my body for several days about a probable hysterectomy. As I relaxed and felt within, peace permeated every cell and fiber of my being. I scanned my uterus with my mind's eye. I sent healing light and energy into my womb and asked my higher self if I needed a hysterectomy. "No!" was my divine answer.

I trusted this guidance and set about realigning my body and fibroids so that I would not have difficulty with them. Over the course of a year, I worked persistently on shrinking the tumors. I rubbed castor oil mixed with lavender oil on my belly, wrapped it in cellophane and applied a heating pad for 20 minutes, 1 to 2 times per day. I ate teeming amounts of fresh fruits and vegetables (no red meat, minimal poultry) and reduced my dairy intake. I had acupuncture and spiritual healing sessions. And most of all, I did forgiveness work to release the thoughts and energies that created the fibroids in the first place.

In Louise Hay's Book *Heal Your Body*, where she describes the metaphysical causes of physical illness, she states, "Fibroid tumors arise from nursing a hurt from a partner, a blow to the feminine ego." She also gives affirmations to support healing.

I started here with my forgiveness work, delving into the hurt that I was nursing from my failed marriage. I had been married for 8 years to my first husband

and never became pregnant. I was frustrated and disappointed on countless levels and thought my chances of being a mother had ended with my marriage at 36 years old. I believed I buried that pain in my body which manifested as fibroid tumors.

I utilized Hay's affirmations and diligently practiced a forgiveness technique developed by Dr. Hew Len called Ho'oponopono where I repeated these four phrases: I'm sorry, please forgive me, I love you, thank you, both out loud and silently while I targeted issues in my life that I wanted to heal. I felt vulnerable and raw unleashing the sorrow I had tried to forget, all while still adjusting to motherhood and recovering from the intense surgery.

During that year, I had extremely heavy periods and cramping in my pelvic region as my fibroids dissolved. Sometimes I would bleed through a super tampon and maxi pad combo within an hour which made leaving the house a scary proposition. I haven't fully diminished the tumors, but they declined in size enough not to be problematic. I'm happy to say that 11 years later I still have my womb fully intact!

SHIFT IN MY RELATIONSHIP TO MY BODY

Before pregnancy, I was physically active—I liked to workout, hike, swim, bike and practice yoga among many pursuits. But after my C-section, my confidence in my physical strength and endurance lessened. My dense fibroids caused the surgeons to cut my stomach vertically through massive muscle tissue, instead of the less invasive horizontal incision along the bikini line. Furthermore, my procedure took twice as long as normal which meant extra tugging and suturing of my innards. By the end, I had a weakened core, considerable sensitivity, and a fear of being touched too hard or often on my belly.

I was so misaligned from the trauma on my body that I looked like I had a muscular disorder the way I carried my frame. Luckily, an acupuncturist was able to help me realign my core, but my abdomen was still very fragile for years.

It's taken me ages and disciplined mind and body training (with tons of stomach crunches) to feel sound in my physique again. Lifting weights and swimming have helped me gain enough self-assurance to venture into recreational ice skating, however, I still don't feel as strong and secure as I did before the birth of my little one.

MY TOP TEN TIPS FOR YOU

Pregnancy and having a baby is an important rite of passage for a woman. It is also a time of extreme emotional and physical changes in the body as you can see. Learning to quiet your mind and go within will assist you in staying peaceful, joy-filled and confident! You will be better able to navigate all the transformation taking place in your body and life.

Having a baby isn't just about biology, it is a spiritual agreement! A baby is a conscious, sentient being. Conscious meaning aware of and responding to one's surroundings; awake. Sentience is the ability to feel, perceive or to experience. Your baby is a conscious spiritual being that has chosen you to be its parent, guardian and way-shower in this life. What a magnificent responsibility you've agreed to!

With all this in mind, I've put together my top ten tips to help you develop a deeper spiritual bond with your baby and your body just like I did. Keep in mind there is no right or one way to do this. Let your intuition guide you!

10. **Be gentle and compassionate with yourself.** Love and honor who you are and your process. Cherish your body temple. Cursing your body adds unnecessary stress and blocks intuition. Cursing the process only pushes away what you truly desire.

9. **Be open and willing.** A closed mind and heart will block intuitive communication with your baby. By remaining open and willing, you will be available to hear messages from above and within.

8. **Meditate regularly.** Meditation helps you to ground yourself and connect with your intuitive nature. It helps you calm your mind and body.

7. ***Ground (anchor) yourself frequently.*** A ship in the ocean drops its anchor to be grounded in one place. You ground yourself to bring your own energy back into your space so that you can think clearly and receive divine guidance.

6. ***Keep your chakras open***. When your chakras are open, energy moves easily, you are able to process information with less effort, and you move fluidly in the world. You need open chakras to communicate with your baby and higher self; to develop your intuition.

5. ***Acknowledge your baby as a spiritual being with consciousness and sentience.*** We are all spiritual beings having a physical experience. Just like people communicate with loved ones who have passed on, you can communicate with your baby that's coming through. It is a

cycle of life—there is no beginning or end to a soul. It is and will continue to be.

4. **Say hello to your baby.** Your baby is excited to talk to you! Say hello and listen for a response. Remember these are intuitive conversations, so pay attention to words or pictures in your head, or feelings. There is no right or one way to communicate. Trust yourself.

3. **Practice listening to and following your intuition.** It's time to go beyond your five physical senses and tap into your sixth sense, your intuition. You have the opportunity to receive higher levels of information than ever before.

2. **Let go of your agenda**. Allow your higher self to guide you. Step out of your ego. Let go of

what you think you know or think needs to happen and let miracles unfold!

1. ***Ask your baby what it needs to be best taken care of in this moment!*** Create a partnership NOW. Intuitive two-way communication opens up infinite channels of possibility between you and your child. You can stop worrying and wondering if you are on track by connecting with your baby and higher self for guidance and instruction.

Enjoy these tips and use them often! Just like the saying goes, "Practice makes perfect," you wouldn't go to the gym once and expect to look like a body builder. The more you use your intuitive muscles, the stronger they will be and the more success you will experience. This process was a life-saver for me—I don't think I would have made it through my high-risk pregnancy without establishing intuitive two-way communication with my unborn daughter. It really works!

IN A NUT SHELL

- If you have fibroid tumors, hang in there! I wasn't on any fertility drugs, I was 41 years old and I had a healthy and successful pregnancy. If I can do it, you can too—my journey wasn't easy, but it was victorious in the end!!

- As I've said, pregnancy isn't just about biology. Our spiritual contract as a family, and my divine agreement to be Mecca's mother superseded all of the physical impediments that occurred.

- Learn to ground yourself and tap into your intuition to find your own divine guidance and inspiration. The Universe is ready and willing to support you.

If you would like support on your pregnancy or trying to conceive journey, you can contact me at SandraJonesKeller.com. I am an Intuitive Pregnancy Coach and Spiritual

Energy Healer. My approach is loving and gentle. I teach pregnant moms, new moms and want to be moms how to develop a deeper spiritual bond with their babies. Not pregnant or trying to conceive? Try a spiritual energy healing session which can assist you in releasing energy blocks that have paralyzed your life. That's it for now, lots of love and light to you!

***

BONUS MATERIAL-PREVIEW OF UPCOMING BOOK

I am excited to share excerpts of my upcoming book with you! The working title is "Tips and Missteps of Modern Day Parenting" which is a series of vignettes about my endearing experiences with my daughter. Take a look…

***

Her Binky Is Her Friend

"The American Academy of Pediatrics recommends stopping "binkies" at around 1 year of age. Some health care providers suggest that parents wean their children from the pacifier once they are mobile, to reduce the risk of fall-related injuries."

Really??

If this is the case, then we were really off track! My daughter sucked on her pacifier while pedaling her tricycle, painting murals, and playing chase in the park. She never had a 'fall-related binky injury' and often resembled an eccentric artist with the paci perched on her lips instead of a cigarette.

Some of my mother friends were disturbed that their toddlers wanted comfort far beyond what grandparents and caretakers thought was appropriate. But by this time, I knew that everything with Mecca was a phase, and that this too would soon pass.

Around 2 ½ to 3 years old, my daughter started grinding her pacifiers to bits and silly me kept replenishing them. We could have bought shares of stock for the amount of money we spent on bah-bahs over the years.

One day I became fed up with binkies: I was done with replacing them, done with pawing sticky floors and dark alcoves to find them, done with washing guck and germs off them, just done!

"Mecca, I'm not going to take your pacifiers away, and I'm not going to try to make you stop using them, but I'm not going to buy anymore. You keep chewing them up so I think you're pretty finished with them. What you have is it. Okay?"

"Okay," she sadly agreed.

Well, just because I was complete, doesn't mean she was. For each paci she lost or misplaced, another magically appeared. She'd unearth them in sofa cushions, under beds, sandwiched between car seat cracks, beneath piles of clothes—freaking everywhere. I couldn't escape those things. She used her divine manifesting abilities to call forth 3 years' worth of abandoned soothers over a few months.

In the end, she contentedly weaned herself off her binky friend. There were no power struggles or arguments, no tears or tantrums. By the time she chomped the rubber nipple off the last one, she was ready to say goodbye to her comforting pal.

https://babygooroo.com/articles/when-should-my-baby-stop-using-a-pacifier

***

And I Really Liked Those Shoes

I don't remember exactly how it all started, but one day Mecca threw a toy at me while I was driving, I yelped in shock, she laughed and a nasty pattern erupted.

When you're 3 years old, annoying a parent is very funny.

Fortunately, she wouldn't do this every day, although her timing was impeccable: like when I was maneuvering through heavy traffic, or waiting to make a left turn from a busy intersection.

I tried reasoning with her. "Mecca, please don't throw things at mommy while I'm driving. It's dangerous and distracting. I need to pay attention and getting smacked in the head or having your toy slam into the windshield startles mommy and I could hit someone. Do you understand?"

Slight nod yes with an underlying sly smile was her response.

I tried getting mad. "Stop throwing things at me!"

Low grade giggles.

I tried being wounded. "Mecca, it really hurts mommy's feelings when you fling your toys at me. Please don't do that."

Blank stare.

So as I changed lanes on the bustling highway with big rigs pushing in on both sides, Mecca hurled a shoe at me. The black ballet slipper crashed into the windshield, ricocheted off the steering wheel, and knocked me in the face. My startled squeal brought roaring chuckles from the backseat.

I grabbed the slipper and was about to toss it to her when I had an epiphany that might end this madness: I rolled down the passenger window, pointed to the window to make sure she saw exactly what I was doing, and heaved her ballet flat out onto the side of the road, all while speeding down the interstate.

Her giggles instantly turned into screams. "No, No, NO!" She repeated as we drove farther and farther away from her discarded footwear.

"I'm sorry honey, but I had to do it."

"My shoe, my shoe!" She shrieked through streams of tears.

"Yeah, I know. And I had just bought you those shoes last week. I really liked those ballet slippers too," I said in my calmest voice.

I finally turned the radio up to drown out her sobbing—she whimpered the whole drive home.

After she calmed down, we had a brief chat about the incident. "Mecca, I'm so sorry I threw your shoe out the window, but I felt like I had to do something drastic to get your attention."

"My new shoes," she pouted.

"Yep, I know. Make you a deal--you don't throw things at me while I'm driving, and I won't throw your stuff out the window?"

"Okay." No sly smirks, or giggles or blank stares, just an authentic okay. And she really meant it this time—she never flung an object at me again while I was sat behind the wheel of my car.

***

He Got 2 Presents, I Got Nadda

I love Christmas! When I was a kid I'd start counting down the days until the 25th on December 1st. I couldn't wait to ride my sleek new bike or play with the beautiful doll I had wanted all year. As a mom, I bask in watching my 8-year-old daughter's face brighten as she rips the wrapping paper off her presents, or proudly passes me a gift she's made for me.

On this sunny morning, Mecca opened her first present, then Thomas opened one from her, and I opened one from Thomas. I took pictures and relished the scene. Then Mecca gave Thomas a second present. I waited expectantly for my artsy gift from her as the presents cleared from under the tree.

She finally said, "That's it!"

My eyes widened—no more presents? Confusion set in. "Where's my present from Mecca?" I wondered.

I watched as they laughed and reveled in their gifts. I smiled a bit even though my heart was aching. I finally went to the bathroom so they wouldn't see me cry.

My sadness and disappointment turned into anger. I looked in the mirror and snapped, "What the fuck! I'm the one who takes her to 90% of her activities. I'm the one who makes her dinner, homeschools her and tucks her in at night, and he gets two presents and I get NOTHING!!"

This diatribe went on for another minute or so. "How inconsiderate, ungrateful and mean…? Wait a minute, Mecca's not any of those things."

I caught my breath. "If Mecca is usually very generous and loving, what happened that she didn't make me a present?" I asked myself.

I washed my face, decided not to ask about my gift until I received clarity, and returned to the living room to be with my family. I put my distress in a box so that I wouldn't ruin the day for them.

Two or three days later I had an 'aha' moment that shook me: Mecca had given me a Mother's Day present which had a cute little stuffed animal with it. One day I was decluttering and gave the animal back to her because I didn't want it to go to waste. When I had handed it to her she gave me a weird look, but took it without saying anything.

Okay, it was time to talk to her.

"Mecca, I noticed you didn't make me a present for Christmas. Can I ask why?

"I don't know", her stock answer to everything.

"Well, I've been thinking about it. Is it because I gave part of your Mother's Day present back to you?"

"Yes," she answered in a small voice.

"Did you feel like I didn't value what you had given me?"

"Yes." Her eyes watered so I knew I had nailed it!

"Come here, I want to show you something."

She followed me into my bedroom. I pulled out a manila envelope marked 'Mementos from Mecca' and showed her a stack of cards and trinkets that I had amassed.

"Honey, I'm so sorry I returned your gift. I want you to know that I love and value all the things you've made for me. See all of this stuff I've saved?"

She nodded yes.

"Mommy had a brain fart. I thought I was being considerate, but I see now how that would make you feel like I didn't care about the things you have given me."

I hugged her. She loosely hugged me back.

"Will you forgive me?"

She slowly nodded yes. We sat for a moment and loved each other.

"Is there anything you'd like to say about it?" I asked.

"No."

I gave her a kiss and she scrambled away from me—relieved that conversation was over. I hoped that I had resolved the conflict, but since she didn't say much, it was hard to tell.

A couple of months later she made me a lovely Valentine's Day present. I almost cried in appreciation.

***

Made in the USA
Middletown, DE
05 August 2018